THE BEATLES!

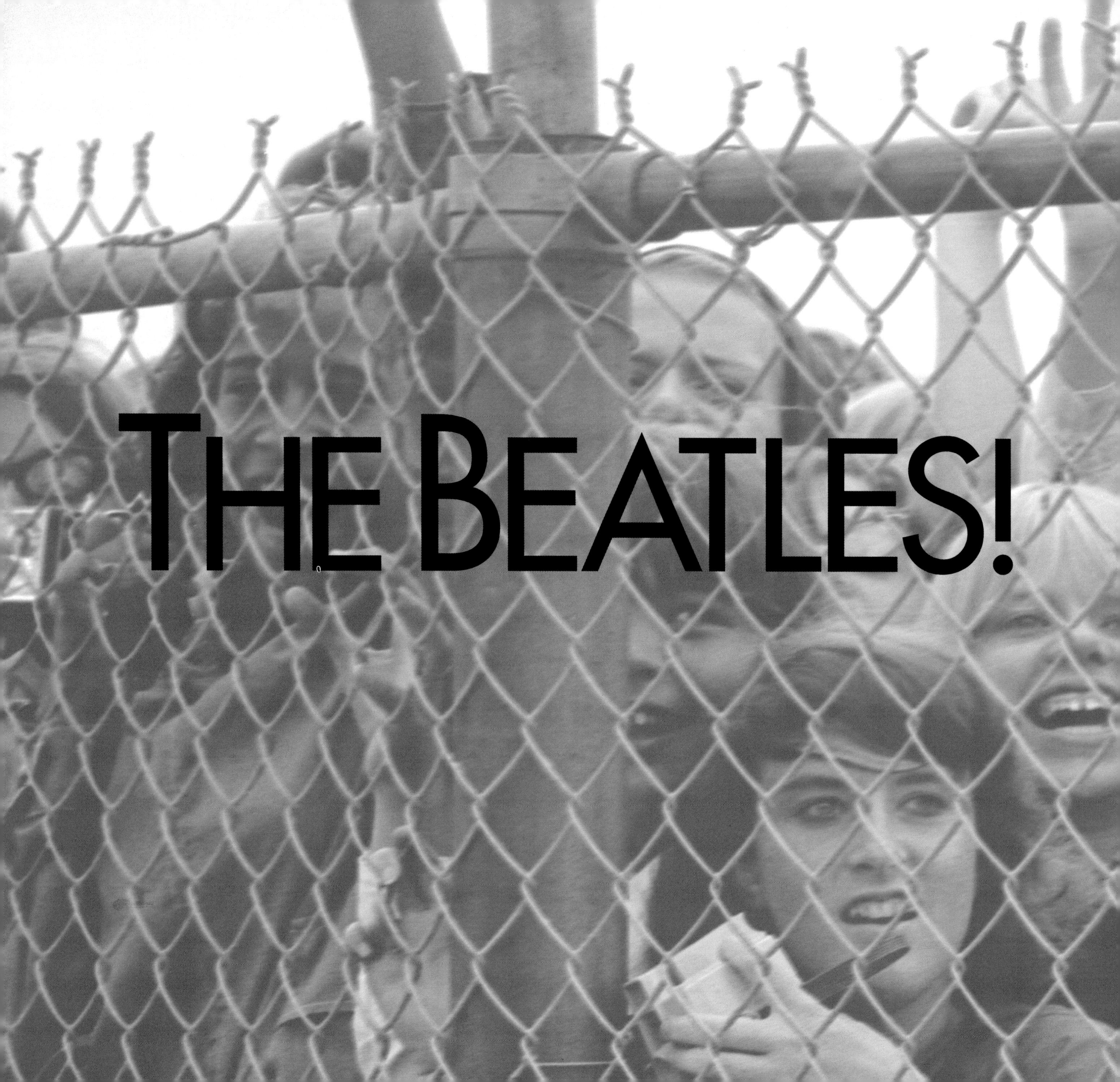
THE BEATLES!

A One-Night Stand

A COLLECTION OF ORIGINAL PHOTOGRAPHS FROM **AUGUST 21, 1965**

Bill Carlson

FOREWORD BY LARRY KANE

JG PRESS

For my fathers—Gene Betz, Jerry Knapp, Merle Morris, Jack Brown, Bill Jenkins, and William Nassif

and

Lois, Tomás, Elena, and Denise, with love

CREDITS

We'd like to give special thanks to the following people for their contributions to this book:

TONY BARROW is the author of *Paul McCartney: Now and Then* (Boutique Editions/Carlton Publishing UK, 2004) and *John, Paul, George, Ringo and Me* (Boutique Editions/Carlton Publishing UK, 2005)

LARRY KANE is the author of *Ticket to Ride* and *Lennon Revealed*. Larry Kane's Emmy Award–winning career spans more than forty-five years, including anchor positions at all three of Philadelphia's network-TV affiliates and the ABC network in New York City.

BILL DIEHL is a former WDGY deejay and *St. Paul Pioneer and Press Dispatch* columnist.

COLLEEN SHEEHY has a Ph.D. in American Studies and is the director of education at the Weisman Art Museum at the University of Minnesota in Minneapolis. She curated the first major exhibition on Bruce Springsteen, *Springsteen: Troubadour of the Highway*, for the Weisman Art Museum in 2002. Her other music exhibitions include *Musicapolis: Seen and Scene, 1965–2005*, an exhibition for the Minnesota Center for Photography and *Bob Dylan's American Journey, 1956–1966* for the Weisman Art Museum.

HOLLY STOCKING teaches journalism at Indiana University in Bloomington.

The wonderful Beatles fans who devoted much time, energy, and purpose in order to channel their memories and impressions of the event for this book.

FOREWORD
BY LARRY KANE

It was quite a journey, or "trip," as John Lennon enjoyed describing it, perhaps offering the illusion that the Beatle tours of America were gliding on something other than jet fuel.

I watched sixty-two Beatles concerts in cities across the United States and Canada in 1964 and 1965, the only American journalist to travel to every stop. In a career of fifty years in broadcasting, it was the most unusual and extraordinary adventure. John, Paul, George, and Ringo were real and special to be with, four young men around my own age who were making their way into the history books, one hit song at a time. The emotion surrounding the tours was a separate scene: girls straining their necks, sweating with an anxious physical tension, eyes locked on their subjects, and tears flowing down their cheeks. The eye caught the scene but how could one genuinely bring the visual alive?

In the coverage of this amazing epic, there was something missing: really good photography. Curt Gunther, a Holocaust survivor, managed to make his way on board the first tour in 1964. Curt was a talented candid photograper who played poker with the "boys." He must have won too often, because Curt did not return in 1965.

Most of the photography was limited to wide shots of the arenas and stadiums, and a few closer shots of the Beatles. I carried a Kodak Instamatic that was ahead of its time, but as you can see in my two books on the Beatles, it was a device strictly for amateurs like me.

Alas, there were few photographs of the faces of the Beatles that correctly and definitively gave the viewer a look inside their souls and outside the wide glare of herds of photographers trying to get closer.

A few years back, I was passing a table at the Chicago Fest for Beatles Fans when I discovered a treasure—Bill Carlson's photography of the Beatles' visit to the twin cities on August 21, 1965. Bill has done something that few have. He has given the world close-up photos of the boys in their prime, because the 1965 tour was the apex of their touring career. Forget the fact that our flight from Minneapolis to Portland ended with an engine on fire and an emergency landing in Portland. Forget the fact that the Leamington Motor Court was overtaken by an army of heat-seeking Beatle fans on the night of August 20th. *Never* forget the outdoor concert at Killebrew's ballyard and the fans' reaction.

Just pause for a second from your memory mayhem and look at Carlson's close-ups. You'll feel as close to the Beatles as I was on all those flights and in all those hotel rooms. I don't know the secret of his magic, but his images are as real as yesterday. Yesterday, as Paul would say, seemed so far away. But when you look at the Beatles and their one-night stand in the heartland through the eyes and lens of Bill Carlson, it all comes back. And let's not forget his immortal pictures of the fans, the police, and the environment that shows you how special it was.

These pictures come from the heartland and from the heart of a great photographer, but they are so vivid, so intimate, that they could have been taken at every stop on the tours.

Enjoy this visit with the Beatles as much as I enjoyed traveling with them, and know full well that you will be savoring the labors of one of a select few photo artists who have been able to capture the moods of joy and wonder that the Beatles brought to the heartland, and to the world.

LARRY KANE
PHILADELPHIA, MARCH 2007

INTRODUCTION
BY COLLEEN SHEEHY

By all measurements, the sheer volume of information on the Beatles continues to grow. A conventional Internet search yields nearly four million websites referring to the Beatles. (Bob Dylan is the next closest with three million; the Rolling Stones are a distant 1.7 million; Kurt Cobain comes in at just over 600,000.) RR Bowker, a book industry resource for publishing data, lists more than one thousand books on the Beatles. The world seems to need the Beatles now more than ever, thirty-five years after the group disbanded.

Bill Carlson's book of photographs from the Beatles' visit to Minnesota on August 21, 1965, adds a new chapter to the Beatles story. He brings to Beatles fans, photography aficionados, and history buffs these previously unseen photographs, documenting a day in the life of the Beatles on tour. The Beatles toured in the United States just three times: 1964, 1965, and 1966. And as former Beatles journalist Larry Kane tells it in his recent book, *Ticket to Ride,* the Beatles were still having fun in '65.

Carlson's *The Beatles! A One Night Stand in the Heartland* brings together strands from many remarkable stories: First, the story of the Beatles themselves as phenomenal artists who changed music and culture forever, enchanting new generations of young ears with their remarkably fresh and creative sound. Second, Bill Carlson's own impressive story, and how he intersected with the Beatles as they convened on that singular day in August. And last, the twenty-five thousand or more screaming, shouting, cheering, swooning, clapping, crying, and singing Minnesotans who were inspired and transformed by what they experienced that day.

While a high school student, Carlson apprenticed with the prestigious photographer Merle Morris, whose studio was an affiliate of United Press International. When the press passes came in through the Telex for the Beatles' press conference and concert in Bloomington (the suburb south of Minneapolis where Metropolitan Stadium, the Twins' baseball home, was located), none of the other Morris staff photographers wanted to see that crazy "kids' stuff." So, Carlson claimed a pass, grabbed his Hasselblad and Nikon cameras, and headed out to Met Stadium, not so much as a Beatles fan but as a photography-hungry youth, determined to seize every opportunity to learn and perfect his art form.

His images show the public face of the Beatles at the press conference as they expertly pose and trade quips with reporters. But Carlson also captures some candid exchanges, such as B-Sharp Music's presentation of a new Rickenbacker twelve-string guitar to George Harrison, a gift that came to mean quite a bit to the Beatle. And for someone who grew up in the Twin Cities, Carlson's scenes of the fans are priceless. They look so young, hardly even teenagers. And to think that you might even know one of these young people, boys and girls, and wonder where they are today, is very touching. His fan shots also put the Minnesota youth on the same footing as those in London and New York, the more familiar scenes of Beatlemania, countering the sense, particularly in 1965, that Minnesota was outside of the cultural hot spots. And Carlson's long shots of the concert stage recall the security that had to be enforced then, when not even photographers were allowed on the field. Images of the crowds in the stands vividly bring back the grandeur of the old stadium, which was torn down in 1985 to make way for the Mall of America.

There are other books by Beatles photographers. Robert Freeman, who photographed many album covers for the group, published *The Beatles: A Private View* (2003). Harry Benson photographed them on tour from Paris to Miami, a collection presented in *Once There Was a Way* (2003). But there is no other book like Bill Carlson's that documents one day, one concert, one place. It was a day that brought high fun and high art to the Twin Cities. It was a day that changed many of us forever. It feels altogether right that Carlson's photographs reconstitute this event and its audience again in 2007, the concert's forty-second anniversary.

We have Carlson's partner, Denise Gardner, to thank for the re-emergence of photographs that had been filed away for decades. During that time, Bill was busy working professionally as a photographer, racecar driver, and cinematographer. Denise recognized the power and historical significance of these images and honed her skills of persuasion to convince Bill to bring them to the public.

I was one of the young fans at the concert that August evening. It was my first concert. (My memories of that event and its ongoing impact on me are described elsewhere in this volume.) As one who experienced the phenomenon of the Beatles, I am grateful that Bill decided to share these special images not only with those of us who were in the stands that day, but also with a worldwide audience. Our newspaper articles of that event, glued into scrapbooks, have yellowed and frayed. But our memories will not fade, their staying power boosted by Carlson's gift to us here.

"Art throws something out ahead, and you gotta catch up," hip hop pioneer Chuck D said at a talk for Black History Month last year. In 1964 and 1965, with their record releases, appearances on *The Ed Sullivan Show,* and tours to such hinterlands as Bloomington, Minnesota, the Beatles threw something out. We still are trying to catch up. Carlson's photographs remind us of those wonderful moments of revelation. Yet his images do not belong so much to the past or to any form of nostalgia as they belong to an ongoing present that continues to inspire, as art is meant to do.

THE BEATLES!

I was fifteen years old and went to the 1965 Beatles concert with my boyfriend, who had to work tons of hours at the local Perkins as a busboy to earn the money to buy the tickets. He surprised me with them, and I was, of course, crazy with joy! I always loved Paul the best, because he was gorgeous and we shared the same birth date (June 18). I remember that it was an evening concert, and we dressed up for the event. Even though we were seated high in the stadium, I felt like I was sitting right on the stage. It was thrilling when the opening act started (Cannibal & the Headhunters doing "Land of a Thousand Dances"), because we knew we were just that much closer to seeing "The Fab Four!" The opening act was actually fantastic. I remember thinking that I liked them as well, simply because I could actually hear them and that they inspired us to dance in our seats. Then the magic moment arrived, and the Beatles were announced! The lights seemed to increase, and the roar of screams filled the air. The screams were deafening! The Beatles came running out and I think they had their guitars in their hands when they climbed on stage. We could slightly hear them over the screams, but it was a strain. That was forty-one years ago, and it seems like yesterday . . . I'll never, ever forget that magic night. Ever. . . .

DeEtta Miller, Minneapolis

Opposite: A young fan reveals her obvious predilection in welcoming the famed drummer.

The day began with the Beatles' arrival at 4:30 p.m. in this chartered Electra aircraft from American Flyers at the Wold Chamberlain Airport (now the Minneapolis/St.Paul International Airport).

Security at the airport was tight for the arrival of the Fab Four. More than four thousand fans waited for a chance to see their idols.

Phil Spector (born December 26, 1940) is an American record producer of the 1960s and 1970s, arguably one of the most prolific producers of popular music. He has worked with a long list of famous artists, including the Beatles, the Ramones, Cher, and the Righteous Brothers. Spector's production credits with the Beatles are extensive. Chief among his notable collaborations with the legendary group are John Lennon's solo single "Instant Karma"; the albums *Let It Be*, George Harrison's *All Things Must Pass*, and *Imagine;* and John Lennon's *Plastic Ono Band.*

Although he had no official business with the Beatles that year, Spector came to the concert that day by virtue of his close friendship with the band.

As a young photographer, I was always looking for opportunities, whether it was political events, sporting events, car racing, or musical concerts. So, that's really why I shot the Beatles, Wally Schirra, and car racing, etc. . . . I went to nearly everything in order to shoot film. . . . You know, I was just a kid goofing around with a couple of Nikons and a Hasselblad. And yet the reality is, these images speak to people, which is great.

BILL CARLSON

I would not have missed those six years working with the Beatles as their Press & Public Relations Officer (1963–1968). Devilish at times and angelic at others, the Beatles were heaven and hell to work with because of their constant mood swings. The pressures and stresses of Beatlemania were high and were no doubt having an effect on them. Part of the stress included having to cope with a series of death threats against them in 1966, which we had to take very seriously.

But when we came to Minneapolis for a one-night stand on Saturday, August 21, they were at their happiest and at their most popular. In 1965 they were still enjoying the thrill of playing the vast stadium-type venues across the USA. Fear and boredom led to the end of their touring era only 12 months later, but at the time of the Minnesota gig (tickets priced at $5.50!) at the Metropolitan Stadium in Bloomington, they felt on top of the world and were genuinely enjoying themselves. Less than a week earlier, the Fab Four had played New York's Shea Stadium in front of some 56,000 fans and

they were still on a huge high from that incredible experience.

We flew in from Chicago by charter flight (a Lockheed Electra), which transported the Beatles, our supporting acts, our management entourage and the group of international journalists and deejays authorized in advance by me to travel with us. Unfortunately the management of the hotel where we stayed, the Leamington Motor Inn, had announced the arrival of the Beatles. Consequently, the place was swarming with fans, night and day, throughout our brief visit.

In each city we visited we did a large press conference attended by both local, international and traveling media people. Oddly enough, the Minneapolis conference was broadcast live in its entirety by a local radio station. That particular day, George was the happiest Beatle of all because he was presented with a new guitar from a local music promoter.

TONY BARROW

Tony Barrow, press and public relations officer for the Beatles, lays out the ground rules to the photographers and media before the start of the press conference. Behind Barrow is WDGY deejay and concert emcee Bill Diehl.

In 1965 I was the entertainment editor for the *St. Paul Dispatch* and Pioneer Press, and had my own Top 40 radio show on WDGY. I was also running a booking agency, booking bands all over town.

Ray Colihan was a local promoter here in the Twin Cities, and he used the name "Big Reggie." I worked with Ray for several years, promoting his dances at Danceland out in Excelsior Amusement Park. I would go out and be the emcee at different dances—usually Tuesday, Friday, and Saturday nights.

He called me in 1964 and said, "Bill, how would you like to emcee with the Beatles?" I said, "What?" I couldn't believe it. And he said, "Well I'm going to 'sell the farm'—I'm putting in a bid for the Beatles to come up here at Met Stadium." And I thought "My gosh, that'd be fantastic," because the Beatles were really riding high then. And so I said to Ray, "Great." Then he asked me, "Could you fly down to Chicago, because they want to meet you beforehand . . . they have final approval. Brian Epstein wants to talk to you and explain to you what they want to be done."

So Helen (my then-girlfriend) and I were flown down to Chicago, and went to the Beatles press conference that morning. That afternoon, we went out by the Chicago Stockyards where the kids were already lining up. And at about two o'clock in the afternoon, we just drifted up there to the Beatles' room in the Ambassador East hotel. We were sort of a Beatles entourage, Helen and I. We sat around with the Beatles and Brian Epstein. We talked, visited, and chatted. But I never once asked them for an autograph. Now, maybe that's why I was tolerated, maybe that's why they let me stay there in that room. Talking with them and joking with them, I found out to my astonishment that they were just like the musicians back home. These guys were totally unspoiled and not at all into themselves.

And then that night, we went down to the Chicago Stockyards for the concert at the Amphitheatre. The management had left instructions that I could be right by the stage. And indeed we were, both Helen and I, right up against their stage. The seats at that venue started only about ten feet away, so the people down there in Chicago really saw the Beatles close up.

Fast-forward to August 1965. Ray Colihan told me, "Now, again, we told you down in Chicago, we don't like these deejays that come out and try to be funny." I said, "Don't worry. We went through this down in Chicago and I'm well aware of what you're expecting." And they said, "And we don't want a lot of self-promotion." And I said again, "Don't worry about that." And they said, "And you must make an announcement in this instance, with this setup, that if any of the kids come pounding out onto the field, out of the stands, and onto the baseball field, the concert will be stopped permanently at that point, and the Beatles will leave."

So that was my unenviable chore of the evening. I have been booed occasionally, usually for a poor joke, but I've never heard boos like that night! When I edged out onto the stage and introduced myself, I got a smattering of applause.

I then made the announcement: "I've got to warn you guys and gals now, when the Beatles come out, we'd love to give them a nice big Minnesota/Wisconsin welcome, but if anybody leaves their seats and comes onto the field, the show will stop at that moment. So please don't try to come on the field. Don't leave your seats. And don't come charging towards the Beatles."

Then came the "Boo!" So I replied with a conciliatory "I know, I know, I'm just doing my job." I've always treasured that moment. I've never evoked such passion from a crowd! And unfortunately, in my case, it was negative.

Meeting the Beatles and being the announcer at the concert was one of the highlights of my life, apart from marrying Helen. When people think of Bill Diehl, they won't say that he wrote great movie reviews or won this or that award. Instead they'll say, "He was the emcee with the Beatles." To be famous because I worked with somebody who was REALLY famous—that's secondhand fame. Well, I don't knock it. I don't knock it.

BILL DIEHL
Master of Ceremonies for the August 21, 1965,
Beatles Concert

ARTICLE FROM THE ST. PAUL PIONEER PRESS
SUNDAY, AUGUST 22, 1965

TEENS TUMBLE FOR MOP-TOPPED BRITONS

Beatles Turn Cities Into 'Shrieksville'

By Donald Del Fiacco

The Twin Cities area was visited Saturday by some strange citizens of another world.

They wore long hair and wide grins and easily were identified as Ringo Starr, John Lennon, George Harrison, and Paul McCartney.

They were the Beatles—alleged muscians.

For those who must know all the details, the spaceship carrying the Liverpool, England, swingers touched down at Wold-Chamberlain field at 4:15 p.m.

Awaiting the most phenomenal and controversial act in show business were more than 4,000 teenagers—mostly girls in their early teens—who could only be described as crazed.

The airport was Shrieksville, U.S.A.

The roar of the crowd was louder than the roar of the plane as it whined to a halt about 75 yards from a tall fence near the old passenger terminal.

Behind the fence—a cyclone fence—was indeed a cyclone.

Little girls—many toting binoculars, cameras and transistor radio—crushed against the fence as the door of the silver ship opened to reveal the head of Ringo—drummer-boy extraordinary.

Many of the youngsters had been at the fence several hours and they could hardly believe that the boys had indeed arrived for their "concert" in Metropolitan stadium—that the announcements of their coming were not vicious lies by teasing adults.

"They're here! What'll I do?" screamed a tiny brunette wearing a huge I'm a Beatle Bug button.

Many girls wept hysterically as the quartet pushed through the mob of newsmen to a black Cadillac parked near the plane.

Two girls fell to their knees and pounded the ground. Others pushed at the fence until a huge pole snapped bringing a horde of policemen.

Four girls charged through the line of police like the troops of Genghis Khan and reached the boys as they were about to enter the car.

The police reached the car at about the same time and the joyous arrival amost turned into a female-style rumble.

"I touched Ringo! I touched Ringo!" shouted a heavy-set young lady as an airport policeman pushed her to an exit.

About six girls at the front of the mob behind the fence sang "We love you Beatles, we love you true" over and over again as the nearly 60 policemen watched uneasily.

A couple of airport firemen stood near a hose, hoping—almost praying—that the kids would stay behind the fence. The hose was not used.

H. R. Mulcrone, chief of the airport safety division, carried a shillelagh. "It's just for walking," he chuckled.

Youngsters waved colorful signs reading "Welcome Beatles," "I Luv Beatles," and "P. S. I Love Paul" as the Cadillac sped off to Metropolitan stadium.

It was a glorious day for those who think young—and the day was not yet over.

Hundreds of youngsters followed the Beatles to the Met and loitered on the parking areas as the four held a "press conference."

The "press conference"—to say the most—was unspectacular. The newsmen were far outnumbered by the Beatlemaniacs.

Three Bloomington policemen carrying 42-inch-long riot sticks escorted the Beatles into the crowded Minnesota room. "We don't use them for hitting, just for holding," explained one of the guards.

The Beatles were cocky—almost arrogant—and veddy, veddy British.

Ringo and John sported tee-shirts with wide red and white stripes and rather shabby sports coats. John proudly displayed a dark blue baseball cap bedecked with shiny medals.

Only Paul wore a suit and tie, and George's hair hung nearly to his shoulders.

Ringo declined to hold up a local publication for the cameramen.

"We don't advertise magazines," he said. "That's naughty, says our manager," added John.

Ringo puffed constantly on a cigaret and Paul fiddled with a huge cigar. They were way out—out farther than astronauts Cooper and Conrad.

Here are some of the more profound questions and answers.

Young blonde: "Are you tired, Paul?"

Paul: "No."

Young blonde, again: "How do you like America?"

John: "It's beautiful."

Disc jockey: "How did you feel about being honored by the queen?"

Paul: "Great, very nice. Those who objected to it were lunatics."

Woman: "Is your hair real?"

John: "It's real. How about yours?"

Disc jockey: "I understand you are friends of Elvis Presley."

Beatles: "We've never met."

Disc jockey: "Is it true Trini Lopez is your favorite performer?"

Beatles: "No."

TV personality: "What kind of cigaret are you smoking, Paul?"

Paul: "It's English."

Young brunette: "Paul, is it true you are going to get married?"

Paul: "No."

Just before the press conference ended, George was presented a guitar and was invited by a young lady to "stay at my house the next time you're in town."

An unhappy newsman offered: "Never have so few done so little to take so much from so many."

The Beatles were rushed again as they were led from the Minnesota room.

It kinda made one want to shout the name of the latest Beatle movie.

The name of the movie is "Help!"

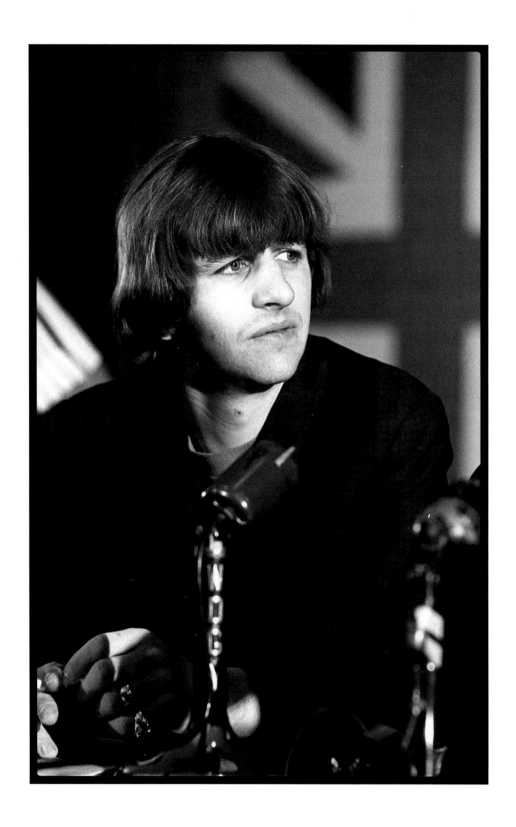

ARTICLE FROM THE ST. PAUL PIONEER PRESS
AUGUST 22, 1965

A SPORTSWRITER?

Twins Interest Beatles' Ringo

By Bob Martel

United Press International

UPI reporter Bob Martel served as a waiter Saturday night when the Beatles were served dinner in the clubhouse of the Minnesota Twins, shortly before an evening performance for 30,000 fans at Metropolitan Stadium.

A group of policemen was in the clubhouse anteroom as I wheeled the cart loaded with dishes, silverware, glasses, and food to the four hungry men from Liverpool.

As I approached the clubhouse door, several of the cops reached for the cart and snatched pieces of silverware from it.

"What's going on?" I said. "You guys are as bad as these kids."

A big fellow with a fork in his grasp reddened, grinned sheepishly and put the fork back on the cart.

The Beatles were relaxing in the clubhouse, the locker room on other days of the American-League–leading Minnesota Twins.

John Lennon peered at a portable television set tuned in to a local wrestling match; Paul McCartney sat in a corner trying out a new guitar;

Ringo Starr and George Harrison lounged on cots which the Twins use for rest between the games of double-headers.

Ringo said he wanted to take a sauna before dinner and asked clubhouse man. Ray Crump if the Twins equipment was available. Crump agreed, but Ringo couldn't convince any of the other three to join him. So they all sat down to a meal of roast beef, mashed potatoes, green beans, salad and milk.

Ringo's chair was stenciled "Killebrew" in large letters, and the drummer showed an interest in the fortunes of slugger Harmon Killebrew and the Twins.

At the request of Ringo and George, Crump produced Twins caps and several autographed baseballs.

"It looks as though they may win," said Ringo.

I helped clear the table and was about to leave when one of the group's assistant-managers held out a $20 tip. I forced myself to decline, and pushed my cart of dirty dishes out the door—straight into bedlam.

It took eight policemen to keep the kids away from the dirty dishes from which their idols had eaten. We battled our way 400 yards back to the kitchen, losing only a few cigarette butts and a spoon or two along the way.

On August 21, 1965, I was one of the lucky twenty-five thousand Minnesotans to attend the Beatles concert at Met Stadium, along with my schoolmate, Marlena. I was eleven years old at the time. When I tell friends, especially younger ones, that my first live concert was with the Beatles, they're astounded, as though I was present at the moment the universe was created.

I didn't scream much myself. I was too fascinated with what was going on around me, and thrilled that I was sharing the stadium with THE BEATLES, even if they appeared about one-inch high out there. It was over all too soon. Nonetheless it marked me. This was not about crushes and infatuation, even though it did have those elements. It was something much deeper and more profound. Eventually my life's work became devoted to understanding art in its many expressions—musical, visual, literary, theatrical—all the elements of the Beatles' forms.

I thank Bill Carlson for sharing his photographs from that magical night and for reviving our memories of an event that has remained mostly invisible in our visual record. His behind-the-scenes shots of the local press conference—not seen before now—remind us that these Beatles events were like performance art. Their charm, their unflappable graciousness, their wittiness sealed our love of these lads, especially in the face of the really ridiculous questions the Beatles were subjected to by the press. In Bloomington, for instance, one reporter asked the absurd question, "How do you sleep with your long hair?" Without missing a beat, George Harrison calmly replied, "The same way that you sleep with your arms and legs." The adult world was utterly flummoxed by them.

COLLEEN SHEEHY

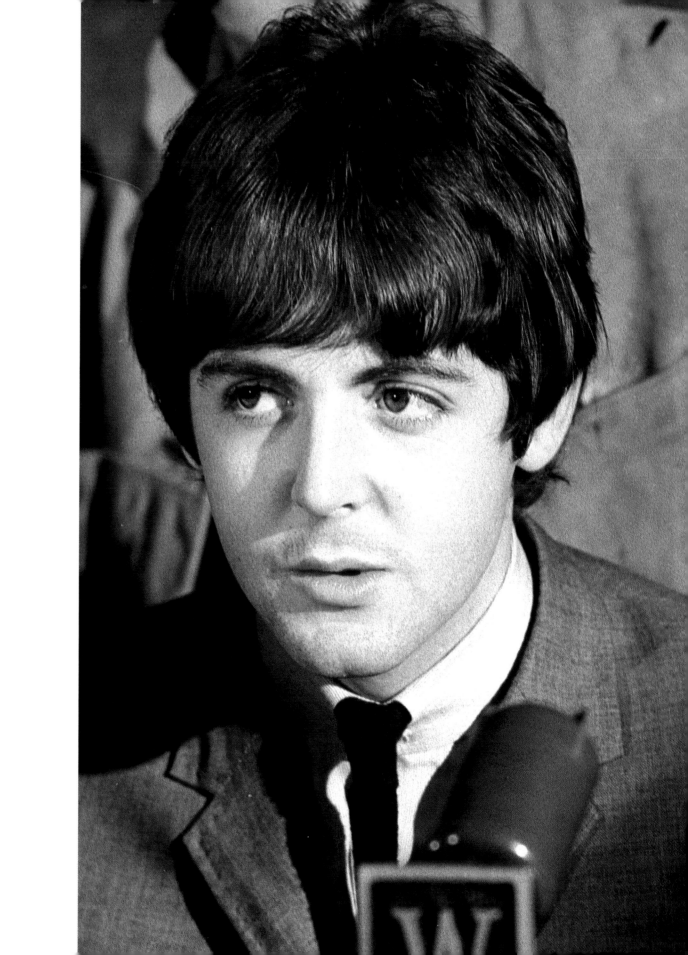

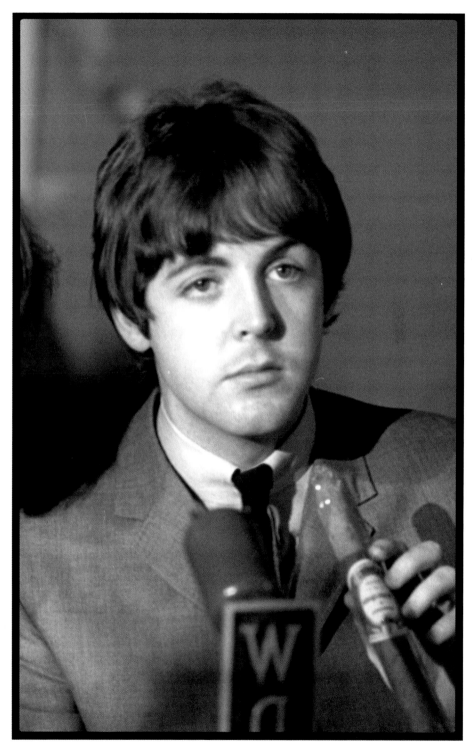

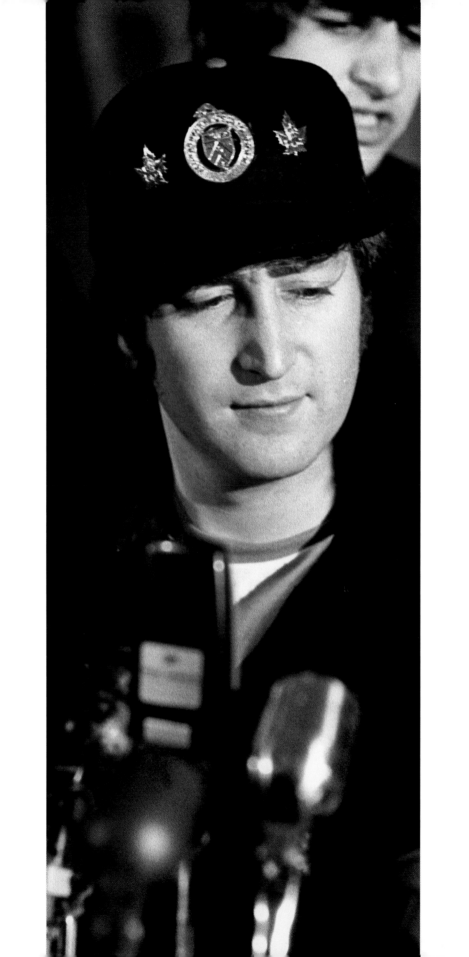

I remember that the Beatles themselves were really relaxed. Also, I think the conference went on much longer than was planned. Because the Beatles were goofing around so much and because everybody was having such a good time, I had the chance to shoot more than I may have shot otherwise.

BILL CARLSON

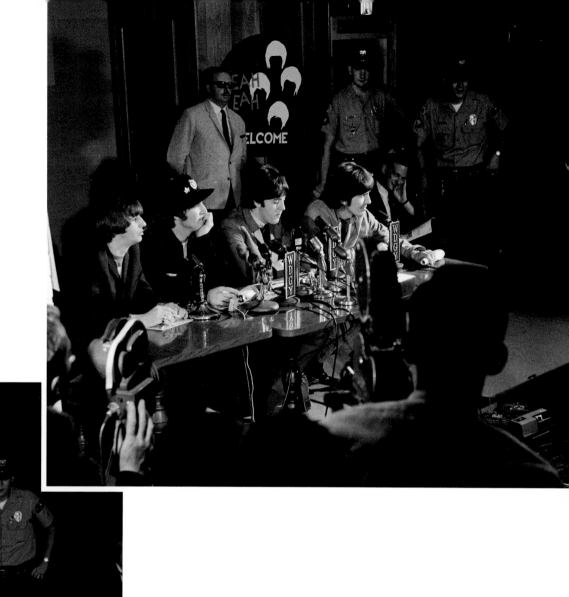

Before everything went digital, there was no "delete" option on the camera. I suppose this was a happy inconvenience, because many of the shots that speak to people today are ones that I would not have selected.

BILL CARLSON

I remember all the waiting for the Beatles concert to begin. I also recall the circulating rumor that if there was too much screaming, the Beatles would leave. It must have been much quieter than what they had experienced at other concerts, because I remember John Lennon moving his arms up and down trying to get us to yell louder when they came out.

DEBORAH MALECHA, ISANTI, MINNESOTA

Looking at Paul McCartney's face in these Beatles pictures brings me back to that day in 1965. I was there at that concert with my little brother. I remember seeing Paul and the boys enter the stadium. Looking at these pictures of the Beatles allows me to relive those magical moments again and again.

TINA J., EVANSTON, ILLINOIS

Randy Resnick of B-Sharp Music presents a Rickenbacker 360/12 to George Harrison.

In a November 1987 interview for *Guitar Player,* Harrison talked about receiving the instrument:

Guitar Player: Did Rickenbacker give you a 12-string?
George: Yeah, I got number two. This friend of mine in England who takes care of guitars, Alan Rogan, just found out that the Rickenbacker 12-string of mine is the second one they made. The first one they gave to a woman, and the second one is the one I got. I got another one from them with the rounded cutaways, but I´m glad to say that the one that went missing—I got a lot of stuff stolen or lost—wasn´t the original one.

The Beatles (especially John Lennon) were my life. I could hardly breathe waiting for the August 21st concert. I carefully planned what I would wear and how I would do my hair. I put my ticket up on my bulletin board in my bedroom, right next to my cherished Beatles pictures and typed-out Beatles lyrics. Every night before I went to bed, I looked at my concert ticket. The day of the concert, I could hardly contain myself. I must have watched that clock all day long.

SUZIE S., MINNEAPOLIS, MINNESOTA

Beatles tickets in hand, we found our seats on the first base line of the stadium. I saw several large banners hanging from the upper deck that said things like "Beatles Forever." I remember a line of speakers along the first and third base lines directed at the grandstands. We impatiently watched the opening acts— The Sounds Inc., Cannibal and the Headhunters and Brenda Holloway. Meanwhile, in the parking lot outside, our parents were observing the feverish Beatles fans trying to hop the fence to get in. Finally, the Beatles emerged from the Twins dugout! It was Paul McCartney, holding his distinctive Hofner bass over-head and John Lennon wearing a cap, both of them headed for the stage on second base. The concert was magical, everything one would expect, and then some. About half way through the show a helicopter flew low over the stadium and circled a few times. It was towing a lighted sign that said "KDWB and B Sharp Music Welcome the Beatles."

KERRY S., TILLAMOOK, OREGON

Police Tell of Ejecting Girls at Beatles' Motel

Minneapolis police reported Tuesday that they rousted several girls from the motor hotel rooms where members of the Beatles entourage were staying Saturday night after their performance in Minneapolis.

"The objective was to eliminate trouble before it started," said Police Inspector Donald R. Dwyer.

Dwyer said some members of the Beatles' traveling party, including one of the Beatles, were threatened with arrest in connection with the incidents.

But no arrests were made, he added, because there was not sufficient evidence of infractions and because those involved complied with police requests.

The Beatle who was involved in the incident was Paul McCartney, according to Dwyer. The other three—Ringo Starr, George Harrison, and John Lennon—were "above reproach," Dwyer said.

Dwyer said police learned Saturday night that members of the entourage had brought girls from nearby sidewalks into fifth-floor rooms of the Leamington Motor Inn, 10th St. and 4th Av. S.

Robert E. Short, owner of the inn, said he understood the youngsters got into the rooms with disc jockeys and newspaper reporters who were traveling with the Beatles.

The Beatles were accompanied by nearly 60 other rock 'n' roll entertainers, reporters, disc jockeys, and stagehands on their visit to Minneapolis. About 30 of the party were registered at the inn, according to motel officials.

The security provided by the motel was excellent, but young men in the Beatles' party got the girls past officials by saying they were members of the entourage, Dwyer said.

"When we became aware of the suspicion of the presence of young girls on the fifth floor, we went immediately to that area to see if the occupants were registered guests," Dwyer said. Those who weren't were asked to leave.

More than 10 girls, ranging in age from 15 to 20, were asked to leave some 20 rooms reserved for the Beatles' entourage, Dwyer said.

He said that when police, acting on information that McCartney had a girl in his room, demanded entrance, they found the door secured with a night chain.

Police called on the Beatles' tour manager to shout to McCartney that he would be jailed unless the girl was out of the room within two minutes.

Dwyer said a young blonde came out within the time limit and had identification to show that she was 21.

Beatles press secretary Tony Barrow could not be reached for comment.

Authorities in Chicago, Ill., where the Beatles appeared before coming to Minneapolis, and in Portland, Ore., where they went afterward, said there were no reports of problems in those cities. The Beatles arrived in Hollywood, Calif., yesterday. They are scheduled to appear in San Diego, Calif., Saturday and in Hollywood Sunday and Monday.

ARE MOP TOPS REAL? YEAH, YEAH, YEAH
By Alan Holbert

The Beatles—most interesting thing about England since Christine Keeler—held a press conference Saturday in the Minnesota Room of Metropolitan Stadium.

It was a 12-microphone and 5-TV camera press conference with about 150 warm bodies crowded into the even warmer, smoke-filled room.

At 5:27 p.m., the Beatles walked into the room led by five policemen carrying wooden sticks 42 inches long.

First was Ringo Starr, still wearing his read-and-white striped polo shirt with a brown coat over it.

Then came John (the poet-author) Lennon with a similar red-and-white polo shirt, with a black long-sleeved shirt over it and a blue cap with three brass buttons on it.

Next was Paul McCartney in a gray suit.

Then George Harrison, who wore a suede coat and jeans.

All of them were smoking except Paul, who was chewing gum.

The questions covered a number of significant topics, including:

Disc jockey: Paul, would you hold up one of these shirts? The disc jockey thrust one onto the table in front of him.

Paul: No.

Disc jockey: Please, my station said I had to have you do it.

Paul: Don't do everything you're told or you'll get in trouble.

Q: George, hold up the cigar.

George: I don't like cigars.

Q: John, how much was your hat?

John: I got it free when I arrived in Minneapolis.

Q: Ringo, what do you think of your fans?

Ringo: The ones who scream and shout are a bunch of idiotic lunatics.

Q: Is your hair real?

George: Our hair's real, lady. What about yours?

Q: What do you do with all your money?

Ringo: We bury it.

Q: When you do a new song, how do you decide who sings the lead?

John: We just get together and whoever knows most of the words sings the lead.

Q: How do you sleep with your hair that long?

George: How do you sleep with your arms and legs still hooked on?

Q: I'm such and so from wonderful rock 'n' roll such and so radio station.

George: How do you do? I'm wonderful George from wonderful WWW.

Q: I understand you're all good friends of Elvis Presley.

Beatles (unison): We've never met Elvis Presley.

After the Beatles, who mumbled to each other and laughed throughout the press conference, had finished putting down all the teen-agers and disc jockeys they ended the fun—but not until one blonde teen-ager stood up and yelled, "If you ever come to Omaha you can stay at my house."

"Yeah, Yeah, Yeah," replied the Beatles.

When people feel the need to ask me my age, I simply reply "old enough to have seen the Beatles play live." In 1965, I was thirteen years old and living in a small southern Minnesota town. When news came across my trusty transistor radio that THEY were coming to Minneapolis, the world stopped. Mom sent away for two tickets (for my brother and myself)—eleven big ones!! When those precious slips of paper arrived at our house, I suddenly became neurotic! I slept with those tickets in my hand inside my pillowcase and prayed every night that it would not rain on the day of the concert. When August 21st came, it dawned bright and sunny. My parents drove us to Minneapolis and dropped us off at Met Stadium. We went right in and the first thing my brother did was buy a hot dog. I remember looking at him and saying, "How can you think of food at a time like this?" I was wearing a plaid skirt with black knee-high socks, a white blouse, and a green v-neck sweater vest. I can still see the huge hand-painted banners that circled the railings of the upper decks. And then I remember them . . . running out onto the playing field, waving and laughing. Oddly, I don't remember screaming, although everyone was screaming. My magical moment was the point where I swear George was looking right at me! In my pocket, I had brought along a pencil and small piece of paper, and with each passing song I scribbled the title down. I still have that faded piece of paper, tucked safely away. It all was quite surreal, looking back on that night now. Saturday, August 21, 1965, was the day that changed my life. From that point forward, I live in a time frame of "before and after" that concert. A long time ago I found a short paragraph written by a fan that I still carry in my wallet. She said, "They are with me every day. They were magic. They still have the power to touch me."

KATHY, MINNEAPOLIS

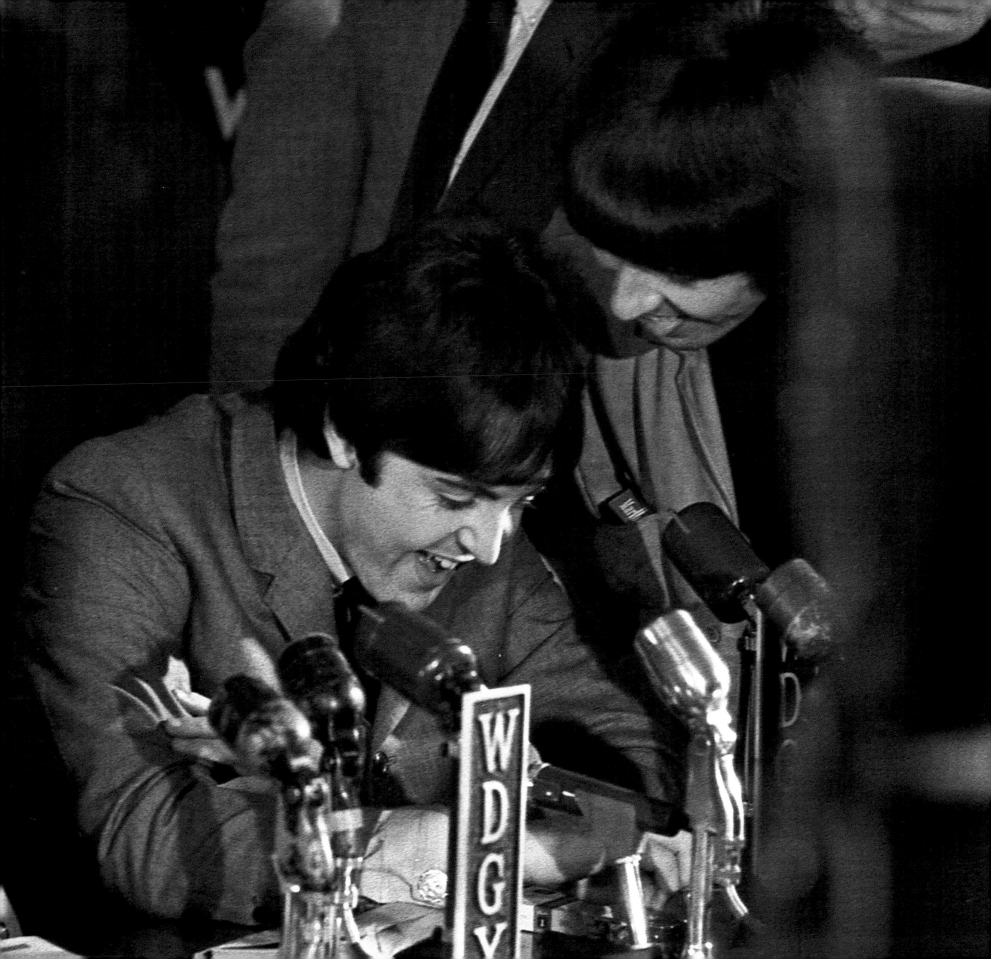

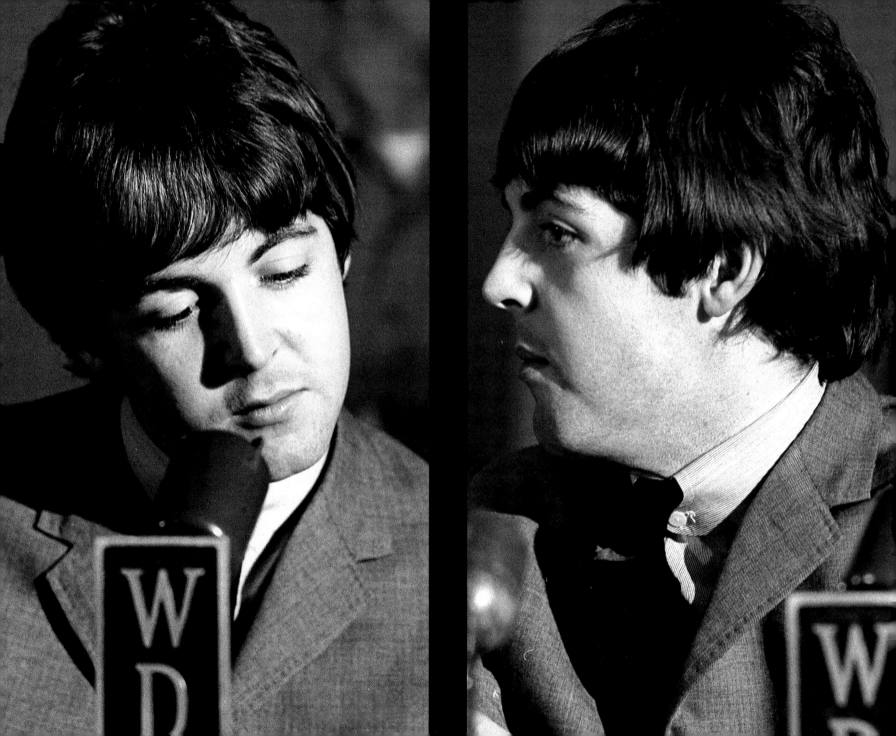

I was at the Beatles concert in 1965. Thirteen years old and, boy, was I in LOVE with the Beatles. Okay, well, mostly Ringo Starr. My uncle had a friend who was working at the concert, and he had an extra ticket. So I went with his two daughters. We were seated ten rows up on the lower level behind the first base dugout. And that's exactly where the Beatles came out onto the stadium. What a moment! They suddenly appeared, turned around, and I swear Ringo waved just at me! That's how close to them I was. They came out and everyone was screaming. What a moment in my life. Looking at the Beatles pictures (well, the Ringo ones mostly!), I can feel myself at thirteen again. I still talk about that concert to this day. I will never, ever forget it.

JULIA D., GLOVERSVILLE, NEW YORK

When I was fourteen, I would stay up late into the night just waiting to hear one of the new Beatles songs. I had Beatles pictures all around my bedroom, which I had to share with three other members of my family. We were a little cramped for space, but we worked it out in those days, because that's what you did.

The concert was in Bloomington, and we lived in the northern suburb of Spring Lake Park. There was no way my folks would have driven us to a concert, especially in Bloomington. So my uncle drove us out to the concert in the back of his covered pick-up truck. Not very elegant but, heh . . . we were going to the Beatles concert! If my memory serves me correctly, our seats were way up in the bleachers, to the right of home plate.

While the seating was so-so, the Beatles were great!!! I remember someone letting me use their binoculars briefly, so I could see them a little better. Wherever you are, thank you!

JUDY B., MINNESOTA

Ringo puffed constantly on a cigaret and Paul fiddled with a huge cigar. They were way out—out farther than astronauts Cooper and Conrad.

St. Paul Pioneer Press

Photographer Bill Carlson guessed that the press conference went on longer than scheduled because the
Fab Four were such friendly and receptive subjects.

INTERVIEW WITH EMCEE BILL DIEHL

Did the promoter, Ray Colihan (Big Reggie), discuss with you his plans regarding promotion of the 1965 Beatles concert in Bloomington?

Yes, and he was afraid to promote. Ray Colihan did this with another act, the Rolling Stones. The Stones came to Danceland, and they could have easily accommodated 1,200 kids out there. Instead, they came out and the turnout was about 350 kids, because Colihan hadn't promoted it. He was scared—he thought the word of mouth would carry it, and it just didn't. But he didn't learn from that lesson, and he didn't promote the Beatles. He was afraid that it was just going to be overfilled to overflowing, and that there'd be all kinds of police trouble. He was really, really worried. Beforehand, I urged him. I said, "You should be running at least a half page ad in the newspaper or something."

How much radio promotion was there?

None. It was promoted only by what you would say, casual conversation.

No radio promotion?!?

No radio commercials. You know, like, "'She loves me, yeah, yeah, yeah.' The Beatles, the Beatles are coming to the Twin Cities!" You know, none of that. And it drove me crazy. Afterward, Ray said, "Diehl, you're right." Nonetheless, he said, "If I had my choice between 35,000 kids out there and 26,000," he said, "I really feel in my heart of hearts I'd go with the 26,000." I think he was scared to death that he'd lose licenses and be sued. He was imagining all sorts of mental scenarios, you know, about the crowd going wild. I remember saying, "Ray, last year we were down at the Chicago Stockyards Auditorium, and there was none of that. The kids came, they yelled and screamed, and then they left!" I said, "There was no rioting." It didn't matter—he was worried sick.

The stadium seated, out there, as I recall, about 35,000. But the crowd that night was just short of 26,000. They kind of played right down the middle, where home plate would

Bill Diehl stands at the far right in this photo.

have been. They were way out there, on the pitcher's mound, and you knew you weren't sitting right on top of these people. I was a little disappointed in that, in that they weren't closer to the crowd.

But they were really fearful . . . that these kids, not knowing the midwesterners (and how comparatively reserved we are), they were really worried about the kids just coming pounding out of the stands and charging up to the stage.

Did Colihan make any money on the event?

He did, he made a little money. He didn't make anywhere near what he could have. He did tell me that he didn't lose. I said, "Are you in the black?" And he said, "Oh yeah, I'm in the black." But he said, "I know I could have made a lot more, but I'll just take the little that I made and be happy with that." He was very philosophical about it.

Was there a lot of discussion afterward about . . .

About the lack of crowds? Yes, and it's interesting that the Beatles considered it one of their poorest turnouts because they were used to playing to capacity crowds. The Beatles had eyes, they could look up to the back, the grandstands and see all these empty seats, and wonder what in the world was happening.

Did you hear them saying anything about it afterwards?

I've got to be honest with you, I might have heard Paul McCartney asking about it, where the crowds were or what happened. But it wasn't made a big issue, because of all the excitement afterward. It's been magnified out of all proportion—when they went to downtown Minneapolis where they stayed overnight and supposedly girls were found in their rooms. As if the Beatles had to, you know, have teenage girls in their rooms for sex purposes or anything like that. It was ridiculous, with the Chief of Police of Minneapolis saying, "I'll never let them in again because of . . ." It was nothing, just maybe a hundred, two hundred kids down there. But to the Minneapolis police, this was practically a riot. They acted like some small village that suddenly had a big turnout.

You were mentioning something about the rivalry between WDGY and KDWB.

KDWB, which was WDGY's rival, went crazy when they found out that I was going to be the emcee, and that there was going to be a press conference broadcast exclusively on WDGY. KDWB wanted to be a part of the show, at least at the stadium, and so Sam Sherwood from KDWB called Ray Colihan, and he said, "Well, you better call Bill Diehl."

And so Sam called me and I said, "Oh, no, this is a WDGY, Big Reggie promotion. We're promoting it and Big Reggie of course is booking it, financing it, and he's tied in with WDGY." So, Sam Sherwood went to Paul Goetz, branch manager for Capital Records at that time here in the Twin Cities, and told him that they better be included in the action at the ballpark. Eventually Sam told him, "If you don't let us on the stage," (and he denies this, but it's true), "If you don't let us on the stage we'll never play a Beatles record again, and in fact, we may not play any Capital records again."

Well, Paul Goetz called me up and he was frantic. So Big Reggie told them, "Well don't put them on the spot."

The thing was, I could have excluded KDWB because they weren't in the American Association of Allied Artists. I was a member of all the unions, which meant that I could go on the stage with anybody and do anything I wanted to, and Sherwood and KDWB didn't have that. So the only way they could get on that stage was to be, technically, working with me, because I was the union representative on that stage. So I finally said, "Well, for Paul Goetz, they can do a brief intro. But no more than two or three lines." And I was the one that made that decision.

KDWB did do one of the cleverest things, in the conference room where the press conference was held. There was a public telephone, a phone booth, at one end of the room, and they got there early and got a man inside the phone booth. And then when the press conference started, they put their nickels in the telephone, and held the phone out trying to pick up Beatles' answers. Somebody was apparently listening to KDWB and said, "How are they getting answers?" Then we looked around and here we saw this guy with a telephone. . . .

He was holding the receiver out, so we went over, and stood around him. When one of our WDGY guys would ask the Beatles a question, we'd all go, "WDGY, WDGY, Weedgy Weedgy," so that he couldn't get the answer. So finally, I think they just gave up!

RAY COLIHAN Presents

THE BEATLES

In Their Only Appearance in this Area!

SATURDAY, AUGUST 21st, 7:30 P.M.
METROPOLITAN STADIUM
BLOOMINGTON, MINNESOTA
— RAIN or SHINE —

Tickets: $5.50, $4.40, $3.50, $2.50 BY MAIL ONLY
Orders filled as received and accepted
only if mailed with stamped, self-addressed envelopes to:

BEATLES CONCERT
Edina State Bank, Edina, Minnesota
Make Check or Money Order Payable to Beatles Concert.

NOTE: All tickets will be mailed between June 1-15.
No tickets can be sold in person, by phone
or at Edina State Bank.

Fans jockey for a glimpse of their heroes as the Fab Four
are escorted from the press conference to the
Metropolitan Stadium.

Ramsey County Deputy Sheriff Douglas Sherry commented to the *Minneapolis Star Tribune*, "I've never seen a mob like this in my life."

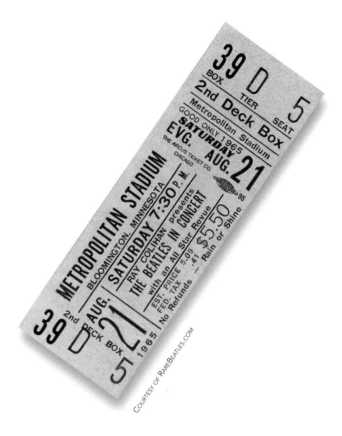

Fans enter the stadium with their tickets, which were priced at $5.50 a piece. The Met Stadium security crew of 150 ushers and police were equipped with smelling salts for the zealous fans.

In 1965, the Beatles second U.S. tour was on the road. The group flew in from Chicago, Illinois, where they had given two shows at White Sox Park the previous Friday. Local promoter Ray Colihan had signed a contract with NEMS Enterprises on March 24, 1965, and had paid a deposit of $25,000 on April 1, 1965, with an agreement to pay the other $25,000 on the 21st of July. This balance was guaranteed against 65 percent of the gross box office receipts. According to the contract, "Additional payments had to be paid by the purchaser to the producer no later than 9.00 p.m. on August 21st." The final contract was signed at the Excelsior Park Ballroom in Excelsior, Minnesota by T. B. Skarning; the local promoter, Ray Colihan; and the U.S. booking agency for the Beatles, the General Artist Coalition. The day after the Twin Cities show, the Beatles flew to the Memorial Coliseum in Portland, Oregon, where they gave two more concerts. Apparently, Carl Wilson and Mike Love of the Beach Boys visited the Fab Four in their dressing room.

The Sounds, Incorporated warm up the crowd.

The Sounds, Incorporated were one of the warm-up bands for the Beatles. From Kent, England, the Sounds made their reputation as a back-up band to American singers visiting the UK, such as Little Richard. A widely respected group, they were among the many artists signed by Brian Epstein. During the mid-sixties, they toured and recorded in their own right, working as session men, and backing-up solo singers on nationwide tours.

Set on the Twins baseball field, the stage was near second base, about forty yards from the closest fan.

EEEEEEEEE!!!

Beatles Draw 30,000 Fans at Met Concert

By Allan Holbert

A crowd of about 30,000 people—mostly squirming, writhing, clapping teen-agers—screamed and screeched their approval of the Beatles Saturday Night at Metropolitan Stadium.

Starting with "She's a Woman," Liverpool's most famous four sang and played 11 numbers that included "A Ticket to Ride," "Everybody's Trying to Be My Baby," "A Hard Day's Night" and other musical masterpieces.

While there were large portions of the songs that you could hear over the frenzied roar, it was impossible to tell what they were singing unless you were sitting by a teen-ager who could tell you the names of the songs.

Actually the screaming about the music wasn't half as bad as the shrieking that was heard whenever one of the boys would wave to a section of the crowd.

The program started about 7:30 p.m. with warm-up numbers (as if they were needed) by such entertainers as King Curtis, Hannibal and the Headliners and Brenda Hollaway.

Then shortly after 8:30 all heaven broke loose when Ringo Starr, George Harrison, Paul McCartney and John Lennon came up out of the Twins' dugout and strolled toward the stage that was set up over second base.

The 150 or so ushers, armed with smelling salts, braced themselves. The 150 or so ushers and policemen, standing guard in front of the box seats armed with 42-inch-long wooden sticks, gritted their teeth.

Overhead a helicopter flashed lights that said "Welcome Beatles," and the crazy, exciting music began.

And as Mary Drewitz, 15, of 4026 Vincent Av. S. said, "Aren't they wonderful, wonderful, wonderful!?!"

Earlier yesterday, some 3,000 screaming teen-agers greeted the Beatles when they landed at Minneapolis-St. Paul International Airport.

They screamed so loud you couldn't hear yourself scream.

You couldn't hear the four engines of the chartered American Flyer Airliner as it taxied to a stop about 4:15 near 61st St. and 34th Av. S.

The screaming pitch rose upwards of unbearable as the Beatles walked off the plane. Drummer Ringo Starr, wearing a red-and-white striped polo shirt and jeans, led the way.

The rock 'n' roll quartet quickly climbed into a black Cadillac limousine and sped off to Met Stadium at speeds close to 65 miles an hour.

While they were getting into the limousine, George Harrison waved to the crowd and smiled, but with his other hand he locked the car's door.

A couple of rather heavy women, who haven't been teen-agers for a number of years, crashed through the police line. They touched Paul McCartney before they were pushed back by a number of policemen and Ray Colihan, the local booker of the Beatles show.

After the Beatles left the airport, many of the teen-agers remained behind the steel fence and cried.

Dolly Fuller, 14, 8725 E. River Road, said she was weeping "because they said they would stay 'til we could take pictures and they just left."

Douglas A. Sherry, captain in the Ramsey County deputy sheriff's reserve, commented, "I've never seen a mob like this in my life. I thought Frank Sinatra was bad. But the mob for this thing has him all beat to pieces."

Signs welcoming the foursome from Liverpool, England, bobbed through the crowd.

"Welcome to the Twin Cities," one said. Another welcomed "John, Paul, Ringo and Geo.," with the postscript, "I love Paul." Still another proclaimed, "The Beatles Are a Girl's Best Friend."

There was pandemonium at the stadium press room when the Beatles showed up five minutes late for a press conference with disc jockeys and reporters.

When they did finally arrive about 5:35, they took another five hectic minutes for pictures, then the questioning began.

Inside the gates, before the Beatles arrived, policemen and ushers milled around—waiting.

"It's going to be a battle," a brown-clad officer said as he glanced toward the packed main gate where hundreds of Beatle-banged teenagers sported "I Love Ringo" buttons, cameras and binoculars.

"Naw, it'll just be another workday," returned an usher.

"Wanna bet? Just look at all those hungry eyes!"

Outside the women's locker room between the Twins dressing room and the Minnesota Room, some 10 teen-aged girls lined up quietly and tensely along the concrete wall—waiting.

"Now, remember," ordered Jess Masener, assistant concessions manager, "You can see 'em if you don't squeal."

The girls, all stadium employees, held their breath. "There they are!" squealed one, clapping her hand over her mouth.

And John, George, Paul and Ringo, led by a club-carrying policeman, sauntered by on their way to their press conference down the hall.

Sandy Olson, 16, 9221 Oakland Av. S., Bloomington, was in tears: "My flash didn't go off!" she sobbed.

"Now settle down," Masener said with a gruff smile. "We've got work to do."

It was 5:50 p.m. in the stadium stands behind home plate.

Usher Jim McCall, 16, 4818 Oakland Av. S., stood by a ramp—waiting.

"Main thing," he said, "to keep things safe."

It was 5:53 p.m. Three hundred and fifty policemen from Bloomington, Hennepin and Ramsey Counties began to spread out across the stands. Ushers checked their personal supplies of smelling salts and took their posts.

It was 5:55 p.m. Gates A, K, and L opened first and youngsters scurried past ticket-rippers, bought Beatles Programs, and scrambled to their seats.

At Gate C, fans chanted "We want in, we want in!" And at 6 p.m., Gate C, then Gate D, flung wide.

They were in!

It was 6:05 p.m., one hour and 25 minutes before the Beatles were scheduled to begin their concert.

Little Billy Berg, 9 Route 1, Wayzata, sat in his box seat and sighed with disinterest.

"Hey, when do we get our hot dogs?" he asked.

BEATLEMANIA—A FULL 35 MINUTES OF IT
Ringo's Smile Triggers Wild Emotional Jag
By Ralph Engerson

A Boeing passenger jet flew rather low over Metropolitan stadium Saturday night—and nobody noticed it.

In fact, few even heard it, for at that moment Ringo Starr had smiled and was waving at 30,000-plus Beatle fans who expressed their Beatlemania in one long bloodcurdling shriek.

For 35 minutes the Beatles played and for 35 minutes the whole stadium full of teenage girls were on one wild emotional jag. All told, 11 songs found their way into the night air.

The stadium's PA system was turned up to the last wall, and occasionally a snatch of Beatle-made music filtered past the first row of fans.

They cried, climbed fences, hung by the bleachers' framing, and stared hungrily through an assortment of binoculars and telescopes at the four entrancing (and very wealthy) men from Britain on stage out past the pitcher's mound.

When the Beatles trooped onto the field at 8:45 p.m. surrounded by a flying wedge of policemen, about 5,000 flashbulbs popped in a blinding staccato as camera fans tried to capture this immortal moment for their scrapbooks.

While the girls (and a few boys) shrieked, the 193 police and 300-plus ushers nervously watched the crowd, hefted yard-long billy clubs (used as a barrier for crowd control) and kept their backs to the Beatles at all times.

"I don't get it," said one policeman watching a trio of blonde teeners weeping in hysterical happiness. "I mean, I like some kinds of music, but it doesn't grab me that much. Only time I ever cried when I heard a song was back in the second World War, when I was overseas in the Pacific and they were playing "White Christmas."

Beatle fans had been tuning up their hysteria for their idols' appearance for nearly three hours, listening to such groups as The Cannibals and Sounds, Inc., the latter group giving an elephant falling-downstairs rhythm to such classics as William Tell Overture and Grieg's Hall of the Mountain King.

Police security during and after this mass emotional binge was very tight. Mayor George Vavoulis, who brought his son and daughter to this historic event ("They said they were scared to drive out here, so I came along.") tried to get out on the sacrosanct field without success.

"Sorry, George," a grim-faced usher said, surveying the mayor's police pass. "It won't work this time."

When the Beatles finally began packing away their bejeweled guitars and drums, the hysteria in the stands redoubled.

As a flying wedge of police rushed the Britons toward the Twins dugout, a wave of humanity began washing down on the thin line of policemen. Other police rushed to their aid, and the line held—barely—as the tousle-headed quartet streaked like fleeing lemmings for safety.

Pandemonium broke loose in the stands as a flood of squealing humanity rushed outside to (possibly) catch the Beatles leaving. Flying cordons of teenagers checked over buses, beer trucks, ambulances, and every other vehicle for a sign of Their Worships.

The search went on for nearly a half hour, during which time the Beatles were speeding down the freeway system to refuge in a downtown Minneapolis hotel.

The Beatles, who are used to such narrow escapades, were on their way just slightly over 30 seconds from the time they disappeared into the Twins dugout.

As a steel door slammed behind them, they hopped aboard a nondescript laundry truck and headed for the gate.

The four bundles from Britain were gone.

I was eleven years old and wanted to see the Beatles more than anything else. We lived in Bloomington, just a few blocks away from Met Stadium, and I was determined to be there for the concert. My dad had a friend who was working at the concert—and this guy happened to have an extra ticket. So I got to go! Lucky me, I sat ten rows up on the lower level behind the first base dugout, right where the Beatles came out. What a moment!!! They came out and turned around and I swear they waved at me. When they came out everyone was standing up and screaming, so of course I started screaming, too. What a moment in my life . . . I still talk about that concert to this day . . . everyone just says "WOW." I will never, ever forget it.

KATHY CORBETT DAVIS, NEW YORK

1965 was a year I never will forget. A local disc jockey, Bill Diehl, introduced the Beatles by saying "a funny thing happened to me on the way to the stadium today. . . . THE BEATLES." I had goose bumps and my teenage heart was pumping. I remember thinking, "So this is how a real rock concert was supposed to feel.

The concert itself ignited a musical energy in me that I never felt before. Looking back, it seems like a dream. I would compare my experience with the Beatles to being a participant at Woodstock. I mean, I was there and saw the Beatles! Since that day in 1965, I have approached music differently. The Beatles combined beat, lyric, and melody in ways that amaze me to this day. Their no-holds-barred way of composing music is seldom reproduced.

I recently left my job in banking after thirty years. And guess what? I am launching a new career as a songwriter. Why the big switch? All I can say is. . . . the Beatles made me do it.

TOM HOPP, COLORADO

I WAS A WAITRESS FOR THREE BEATLES

By Susan Stocking

I didn't faint. I didn't scream. I didn't even squeal.

I ate potato chips.

In a room with Beatles Ringo Starr, George Harrison and John Lennon—and all I did was munch potato chips!

And nervously slop coffee in their saucers.

"Half up," said Lennon, sprawling on the blue spread of a bed in Room 528 of the Leamington Motor Inn. "I drink it white."

It must have been 9 p.m. Saturday while the Beatles were still bugging the crowd at Metropolitan Stadium when I slipped into a waitress uniform and began the long wait in the tiny kitchen of the motor inn.

After 10 p.m., the order from the fifth floor Beatles headquarters finally came in: one medium rare steak sandwich, two trays of assorted sandwiches, seven glasses of ice water, seven coffee cups, a pot of hot water and one of coffee, a bowl of teabags, three small pitchers of milk, a dish of sweet pickles, and chips.

Tray in hand, I tottered behind a waiter with his cart and ascended by freight elevator to the security-tight hideaway.

And there they were, living, breathing, moppy: Lennon sitting cross-legged on the bed near the window and wearing a blaring yellow sweatshirt, Harrison in a black knit T-shirt wandering aimlessly up and down in front of the light mahogany bureau—a pocket radio hugging his ear, and Starr in his red and white polo shirt ushering in the food.

But where was Paul McCartney? "He's ringing home," said Lennon, and he lit out for the coffee pot.

"May I pour," I blurted, biting hard on a potato chip that I'd picked up without thinking.

For an hour and a half, I sat and poured and munched and listened to the visitors from Liverpool banter across the small, blue-walled cubicle.

On 4th Av. S., five stories below, "We want the Beatles!" chants drifted throught the draped windows. No one seemed to notice.

"A reporter in a waitress uniform, eh?" Harrison smirked. "How original."

A Beatle with a sense of humor, eh? How refreshing.

"Hey, whose food is this anyway?" asked Starr, chomping into the $3.75 tenderloin steak sandwich on the cart. "We didn't order any food, did we George?" He plopped onto the double bed next to the door, shrugged as if to say "who cares?" and licked his fingers.

(Must have been ordered by one of the 30 members of the Beatles' official party on the floor, I thought.)

On the television set, sound off, a horse was dragging a cowboy through the dust.

"Aw, c'mon," grumbled Lennon, "they did the same thing last show back!"

Harrison, his radio roaring a Cannibal and His Headhunters tune, growled something about "those bloody DJs."

"Thot's a lie, whot they tell the kids about us playing longer if they're quiet," he said. "We play the same 35- to 50-minute show no matter whot."

"Yea," added Lennon. "And when the audience screams so loud they can't hear us, we just wave more."

I asked Starr if his shirt was the same he'd worn at the concert.

"Whot d'ya mean?" he replied. "Same shirt I've worn all week!"

Then I asked where they'd be headed next morning.

"On to Portland or somewhar," one of them said. "I don't know."

"Fact is, we never know whar we're at," Lennon added, pouring a bag of sugar into his coffee. "Take on the way over here in that truck, for instance . . . I forgot where I was, but I didn't dare ask anybody for fear of hurtin' their feelin's!"

The Beatles made their escape from Metropolitan Stadium in a laundry panel truck, sneaking into the motor inn by way of the basement.

"But don't you ever go out on the town to see the places you're touring?" I wondered.

"Who'd want to see a bunch of statues?" Starr mumbled.

"But Minneapolis has a bunch of lakes," I countered.

"See one lake, you've seen 'em all."

Starr and Harrison sauntered out of the room without saying goodby.

"They're ringin' home—like Paul," Lennon explained. "I'd ring home too, but my wife's in Libya visiting her brother . . . You can't ring Libya."

He sipped a glass of honey ("The manager says my throat's raspy"), struck a match to his Marlboro cigarette and watched a TV detective get stabbed in the stomach.

He told me how the Beatles "beat each other down" if one gets cocky; how even when they're not "in the mood," they quip in public to avoid being labeled "swell-headed," and how their managers normally set up five or six "escape gimmicks" to evade the mobs when they're on tour.

He told me about other things too: about the "greenness" of England, the greatness of rock 'n' roll, and the goodness of knowing what you're talking about before you criticize. (He was referring to the Beatles' critics.)

"You know," he mused, "those kids out there on the street . . . they always find out where we are . . . They're clever, some of 'em."

A "We love you Beatles" song struck up off-key and someone shouted, "We know you're up there Beatles . . . Yea, yea, yea."

I asked if the noise would keep him up that night.

"I can sleep through anythin'," he said. "Think I'll beat it to bed after this cigarette."

I got up to leave. He walked me to the door.

"Cheerio, now," he grinned. "And let me shake your hand like an Englishmun." He gave my much-calmed hand a solid shake.

It was going on midnight. Outside, a police speaker boomed, "O.K., now let's go, everybody home."

At 10:55 a.m. Sunday the Beatles would whisk out the front door—past another crying, yelling mob—and head for the airport in a big black limousine.

Their destination: "Portland or somewhar."

REMINISCENCE BY HOLLY STOCKING,
THE JOURNALISM STUDENT WHO POSED AS A WAITRESS FOR THE BEATLES

I would have been twenty years old when the Beatles made their second trip to the States and this particular visit to the Minnesota heartland. I was a rising senior at Northwestern University's School of Journalism, and a summer intern at the *Minneapolis Tribune.* This was my first big newspaper job.

I'm not privy to how the assignment to cover their visit came about, but City Editor Stu Baird must have identified me as a college student who was hip to the Fab Four and might be interested in doing a story the older guys on staff couldn't, or wouldn't, do.

No one was getting interviews with the Beatles, though, and my editor knew it. He did know where they were staying, but no one was being given access. Radio DJs had reportedly rented rooms on the floor below where the Beatles were staying, to record the sounds of their footsteps, and let audiences in on every imagined squeak of their shoes. Fans had begun to gather on streets outside. Despite the obvious obstacles, my editor asked me to go over to see if I could get in and get something for the paper.

Remember this was my first big newspaper job. I began to wonder how in the world I would do this. Worried, but also excited, I began fantasizing the weirdest things, like sending up balloons from lower floors with a request for an interview, wacky things like that.

My editor must have realized how unsure I was or how painfully sixties my ideas for getting a story were going to be, for at the last minute, he tapped an older reporter—Jerry Kirshenbaum, who later went on to write for *Sports Illustrated*—to go over with me. Jerry somehow knew the manager of the motor inn, and so he talked with the guy and convinced him to let me dress up as a hotel waitresses and carry up any food ordered from the Beatles' floor. I remember going to the kitchen and changing into this ugly, mustard-colored uniform, and waiting for the Beatles minders to put in an order.

Finally, after what seemed like hours, the order arrived. Along with a fellow who actually worked at the hotel, I took an agonizingly slow ride up in a back elevator to where they were staying. My heart was pounding wildly.

The rest is pretty much as I wrote it (see pages 110–111), though one of the first things Ringo Starr did was take one look at my badge and snort. The little plastic badge on my uniform read "Donna Brown," and Ringo made some wisecrack—I don't remember what, but something like what kind of name is that? Whereupon the hotel guy I'd gone up knifed me in the ribs with his elbow. Tell them what your real name is, he said. So I blurted out the truth—my real name and my real reason for being there.

At that point, I didn't know whether I'd get thrown out or not. But someone must have taken pity on me because as I began to ask questions and I began to get some answers. My biggest challenge was that I hadn't gone up with a reporter's notebook. I couldn't take notes. So I had to try to commit everything to memory, which was a real challenge because I don't have a very good memory to begin with. But I looked hard and remembered as much as I could. And at one point, after Ringo and George had wandered from the room, I asked John if I could call in a photographer. Sure, he grinned, and so I called the paper, and not long after, a Trib photographer arrived and snapped some photos. Soon, with my deadline looming, I bid John goodnight, racing to another room in the hotel, where I quickly scribbled down every little detail I could recall.

I had to then write the story, which was a huge challenge for someone just starting out. But pumping with adrenalin, I somehow managed, and the story ran on the front page the next day, with the photo of John sitting at a table, looking up at me and laughing while I nervously slopped coffee everywhere but in his cup. I still have the glossy print of that photo somewhere, though I honestly couldn't tell you where.

These days I teach journalism to students who are—unbelievably—the same age now as I was then. Most of these kids grew up with *Yellow Submarine* on their baby boomer parents' stereos and are wild for the Beatles, especially John. Most of them think I'm nuts for not having framed that photo and put it up in my office. They also think I'm nuts when I tell them—in the media ethics class I teach—that now, in this paparazzi-saturated culture, I would not dream of participating in an undercover caper like this one. I didn't think when I was their age about the ethics of dressing up as a waitress to get an interview—no one did—but I now believe celebrities who seek their privacy ought to be allowed to have it. This isn't an issue in the public interest that demands undercover methods. It's just an attention-grabbing feature story.

That said, I have to admit to my students—and to myself—that this was an experience I treasure. But not just because I was—and maybe still am—a little star-struck. What has stayed with me most is the memory of John, an exhausted performer who didn't make snide or belittling remarks when he learned I was a reporter, but took an hour and a half out of his precious "down" time to help a kid get a story. That more than the glamour and glitz of it all is what I'll always remember, the unexpected—and absolutely unnecessary—kindness of a performer who has since then grown larger than life.

HOLLY STOCKING

The Beatles trip to Minneapolis in 1965 was a whirlwind. The Leamington Motor Court (where the Beatles stayed overnight) was inundated with fans—in the hallways, in the rooms and mostly in the stairwells. The hotel was wild, unruly and crazy with emotion. As I remember it, the night of the concert at the Metropolitan Stadium was beautiful. And the Minnesota crowd, contrary to their midwestern reputation, went berserk as was typical of Beatles fans across America. In fact, we had an especially hard time getting out of the stadium area because fans were trying to block the car. Before we left for Portland, I marvelled at the sun setting over the stadium, and so did the Beatles, who were unaware that the flight to Oregon would end in an emergency landing because of an engine fire. All in all, the plane descended safely, and the Beatles, especially John, wished they had never left Minneapolis.

LARRY KANE

The Beatles set list, in order, from the August 21, 1965 concert:

Twist and Shout

She's a Woman

I Feel Fine

Dizzy Miss Lizzy

Ticket to Ride

Everybody's Tryin' to Be My Baby

Can't Buy Me Love

Baby's in Black

I Wanna Be Your Man

A Hard Day's Night

Help!

I'm Down

It was long ago, but I will always remember the thrill of seeing the Beatles live in concert at the Met Stadium in Bloomington, on August 21, 1965. I was fourteen years old, and I had been a fan ever since they were on the *Ed Sullivan Show* in 1964. I know that sounds just like everyone else's story, but that night really made music history for all of us in the USA. We were all changed in those few short moments. It truly was a British invasion!

In the '60s every teen in the Twin cities listened to either WDGY or KDWB for their favorite Beatles music. It was so exciting that the Beatles had included Minneapolis in their 1965 U.S. concert tour. The night of the concert my younger brother, twelve years young at the time; my cousins; and I were all very excited to see the show. My uncle drove us out to Bloomington and, because there was so much traffic and congestion, dropped us off across the highway from the stadium. We were all really too young to be attending this big concert on our own. Looking back on it now, we wonder how we ever managed to orchestrate the drop off and pick up without cell phones!

I remember that it was a really nice warm summer night, and the kids in the stands were all very chatty and excited. I can still remember the great roar of the screaming (me included) when the Beatles took the stage and started to play. It was wonderful, exciting, and very cool to be a part of it. Our seats were in the upper deck so it was hard to see them; they were pretty tiny from up there. But it was, after all, the Beatles, and what a thrill for all of us!

I have continued my love for all things Beatles, and British, through the years, and was inspired to re-create a bit of Liverpool, and the Cavern Club, with artwork, memorabilia, books, records, and collectibles in my family room downstairs. It has been great fun for me.

In 2005, my sister-in-law Jan and my high school friends and I made a Beatles pilgrimage to Liverpool. We took a trip down to London to visit the Abbey Road Studios, and had our photo taken on the famous Abbey Road crosswalk. We wrote our names on the Abbey Road Studio's whitewashed wall, just like all of the other tourists, and signed it, "Fans forever" and "In My Life 1965 Bloomington, MN USA." And so they have been, and always will be. She loves you yeah, yeah, yeah!

JUDY B., MINNESOTA

INTERVIEW WITH AUTHOR BILL CARLSON

How did you come to photograph the Beatles that day in 1965? Was it an assignment you actively sought out?

In 1965 I was seventeen years old, working for a photographic studio called Merle Morris. Merle Morris Studios was associated with United Press International. We were in their system to call in case there was something that they wanted to be shot in Minneapolis. And in August 1965, we got the press passes for the Beatles by telex. As I recall, no one was interested in going and shooting them. The other photographers that worked at Merle Morris were much older, and the Beatles were probably not considered to be very special by the older generations of the time. Moreover, I really didn't even know that much about them myself. I was more of a jazz and classical kind of kid anyway. But I had heard of the Beatles and I had seen their *Ed Sullivan* appearance. So I thought it would be a very interesting subject to photograph. I asked around the studio and nobody wanted the press passes, so I and another young photographer, Don Getsug, went out there and did the photography—and we just had a great time. But it was one of those things where I never found any venue for the photographs, and they basically sat in my files for many years.

So you weren't even a big Beatles fan at the time?

Not really. I became a solid fan of the Beatles with *Sgt. Pepper* and the *White Album.* But I must say that it was only after I met them did I really begin to listen to their music. All four of them were very warm, friendly, and open. That's what struck me the most. They were just good, ordinary guys and they appreciated where they were. Generally speaking, a lot of rock stars don't behave all that well—even in those days. For instance, the Rolling Stones visited Minneapolis shortly after the Beatles did, but they had this bad boy image—the opposite of the nice and friendly boys from Liverpool, England.

What was the atmosphere like, being in the same room as them? Was it as exciting as most of us would imagine?

Yes, it was very pleasant and a lot of fun. All of the photographers and cameramen were laughing and smiling because it was a genuinely fun experience. And Tony Barrow, the press officer, laid down the ground rules of how people would ask questions. He was firm about how things were going to be done. But the Beatles themselves were really relaxed, and I think it went on longer than normal because everybody was having such a good time. Usually, they'd hustle them in and out. But the Beatles were goofing around so much, and everybody was having a great time.

I understand that you spoke with George Harrison—what were your impressions of him?

During the presentation of the Rickenbacker to George, from B-Sharp Music, everything became chaotic as everyone in the room was standing up and wandering around. At one point I got shoved into George Harrison, and all I could think to say was: "Nice guitar." And he looked at me, smiled, and said: "Lovely!" And that was it. I couldn't think of anything else to say to him! But I think my real impression of him is that he was so young, kid-like, in his appreciation of this special gift from B-sharp. It was almost like George and the others had no idea how bright their futures were.

It seems as if, over the years, every photo ever taken of the Beatles has surfaced. How did your images remain lost for so long?

I think I really got distracted. I left Minneapolis in March of 1967 to work for Camera Hawaii, and then I started freelancing for Time Life. From there my life changed completely. Photographers typically look toward the *next* image and not the last image. And if you sold an image to an editor, magazine, or advertising agency, terrific. But at that point you just move on. It's very hard sometimes to think about the historic relevance of what you have done.

Basically, photographers are always thinking about shooting. Not much about what they've done before. My career has been very unusual and on the fast track in the sense that I get so involved in the projects I'm doing that often, a lot of the things that I shoot will perhaps not be fully realized, you know, unless there is a real interest in them. Once the project is done it goes on the shelf and you're on to the next project. But this is fun for me to look back on some of the old archives. It's especially fun when people enjoy them.

Having witnessed such icons up close, what were your general impressions of them? Did you experience anything that went against the general public perception of them?

The one thing that impressed me with the Beatles is that these were just really great guys—relaxed and not arrogant. Most people might assume that they are a certain way because of their celebrity. But honestly, these were real people put in unreal situations.

You chose to be at the Beatles concert on your own time, with no real goal other than to just take pictures. Didn't that strike you as odd? Here are all these kids your age screaming to see the Beatles, dying to see the Beatles, and you were there merely exercising your art?

Yeah, I guess that's probably the way it was. The fact is, I was a musician at that time. But I wasn't in a rock band; I was in a brass band where we played trombones, trumpets, and French horns. We supported rock groups, meaning that rock groups would rent us. We were like the geek squad—we had short hair and we were dorky, but we kicked ass in terms of playing brass. And so rock bands at that time didn't really fascinate me—I was more interested in jazz and orchestra.

But what I was looking for at that particular point in time was to shoot anything, because my goal was to be a photojournalist and to work for *Life* magazine, *Time,* and *Newsweek.* Luckily, at various points in my life, I did. Because I wanted to be a photojournalist, I photographed everything. So I captured it all, from motorcycle races to car races and jazz concerts, because that was my job as I saw it, to record life. And it was a wonderful experience, and I'm glad that as a kid I did it.

When you look at those pictures today, are you proud of what you see?

I think that's a really good question. I'm really happy that people like the photos because others usually find things there that I never found. Maybe I found things in the photographs instinctually, in that I wasn't aware of what I was finding. I look back at some of the photos now and I say, "Wow . . . you know, that dumb kid at seventeen had a pretty good eye." There are so many photos that I probably would have deleted and not printed, and yet these are the images that people have really found great value in.

My job as a photojournalist is to come back with the information and let the editors or the public decide what they really like. And that's what I love about this process, in that other people locate the images that mean something to them. My job is merely to go and gather the images. And in my work with motion pictures now, that's exactly the way I work. I go and gather the images and work with a producer, editor, and a director to really decide as a team what images are significant.

If people call my work "art," I feel blessed. I never really looked at myself as an artist. I've looked at myself as a craftsman, and I've looked at myself as a contributor. I feel that I can create art, if I contribute with other artists. That's something that is really meaningful to me in the sense that, if I'm working with other people who are on the same page, and we're really working toward a goal, I feel that I can be a contributor to art. But an "artist"? I'm just a little uncomfortable with that terminology. In film and video, I feel that I work in concert with so many other artists, and what we come together with is art. So, in that sense, I'm a collaborative artist.

With photography, I stole the moment. I was like Cartier-Bresson, except Cartier-Bresson was using a scalpel and I was using a baseball bat. But I've always said that I'd rather be lucky than good.

How did you transition from still photography to motion pictures?

I think that in some ways, still photography left me.

What do you mean by that?

The digital format—it's amazing technology, and I really admire it to some degree. The fact is that I started as a film photographer, and I still think in film ways. Basically, it is very hard for me to think in terms of the digital format, with digital filmmaking and with Hi-Def. But with film itself, I kind of have the "chops," you know, because I started doing that forty years ago.

I think that the delete factor with digital still photography is a real negative, in the sense that you will likely delete images that people will relate to. And I think that's what occurred to us when we explored putting together these Beatles images. There are a lot of images that I probably would have deleted and yet obviously couldn't delete because of the film format. With film, you expose one negative after another, and like it or not, they're still in your negative file. And so, it occurred to me that some of those images that I would have deleted really appeal to people and really speak to people. I think that my relationship with digital photography is probably different, simply because I came from analog photography.

How did your photography change over the years?

The change for me probably came in Thailand in the early eighties. I spent a lot of time in a refugee camp in Thailand. And it probably made one of the biggest changes in my life. For me, photography was always about What is out there? What is photography? What can I photograph? or What can I represent? Looking back, I see that as very selfish. Spending my time in Thailand in the Hmong refugee camps, I really decided where I wanted to go with my life. I stopped looking *at* people and started looking *with* them. I tried to look at what they were looking at, at what they were seeing, and at what they were feeling. Before this, I was selfishly looking at them.

And I try to do that today, though not always successfully. But I try to look *with* people and not *at* them. And if I can successfully see with them, and help them explain what they are seeing to a wider audience, then I've done my job.

What do you think when you look at your early work?

It's almost like I am my own son. Sometimes when I look at these photos, I see immediately how I was so motivated. The truth is, I had so many good teachers and great mentors in my life. I look back at some of these images and say, "What?! Who's this? How did you figure this out?" The answer is: Because I loved the work. I simply loved the work.

I had great mentors; I had geniuses who were mentoring me. And that just goes to show you how tremendous the impact is when you have some people in your life who really care about you. I had people pushing my buttons every day. I had Merle Morris, who was a genius. I had other people in my life always challenging me, and challenging me in a way that made me want to grow, but not in a way that was frustrating, frightening, or restrictive. They always said, "What's in that stuff? What are you going to do next?"

I learned from the best. I absorbed everything. As a kid, I read photo books and photo magazines every night. In a lot of ways I emulated some of the great photographers of that time, in that I would find something that would speak to me. I would try it, but not always successfully! But I would at least try it. I probably still am a still photographer from the sixties.

I think that if I would say anything to a still photographer today, it would be, "Shoot what you must. Shoot what is most important to you." I think that is probably the most important thing, is to shoot what's important to you, and not shoot what you think everyone else will respond to. Because if you're a professional photographer, you'll have to do this, you'll have to shoot what's important to other people. Of course, that's part of being a professional. But you need the time to recharge your batteries. You need the time to shoot what you must.

Do you have a favorite among the Beatles pictures from that day?

You tend to get into a situation where you like what others like, and so the pictures that people tend to compliment you on tend to stand out in your mind and I think that they'll probably stand out in the book. I was lucky to be there that day, and it was kind of a passing thing, a ship in the night for me. But the images certainly speak to people.

But to your question, one of my favorite photos is of a cop who is looking so disdainfully at the Beatles. The point is that you don't always know. And I think that's the message of that photograph. You just don't know where these things in life are going to go, and you have to open yourself up and be aware.

I didn't become a fan of the Beatles until three or four years after the concert. And I remain a big Beatles fan today. However, it was a big deal for me to go and take the photographs, and I'm glad I did. I was happy that I had been there.

Out of all the photos in your collected works, is there any one that you're most proud of?

I tend to discount my own work. I know that I am my harshest critic, which is good because you tend to closely edit your own photography. Many of the pictures that people have bought are ones that I haven't related to or wouldn't choose as my favorite. And while it's enjoyable to look at the work that I did forty years ago, the images that I am most proud of are the ones that I have done recently. My work in Vietnam, the Yucatan, Peru, Russia, New Guinea, and with the Hmong in northern Thailand better define who I am today.

What motivated you to become a photographer?

It might be easier to ask me, "How did you start breathing?" (Laughter) I was never a jock, and so that's probably why I went into photography. I was a lousy football player—luckily, I found that out early! But photography came to me in a very unlikely way, through my love of the underwater world.

I learned to dive when I was ten, and then when I was twelve or thirteen I got a job, not a real job, because they paid me cash under the table, but I got a job at Midwest Skin Diving. Gene Betz, the owner, was a very accomplished commercial photographer. When I first started working there, I was interested in taking pictures underwater because of my fascination with diving. And Gene taught me how to do that. He taught me how to take pictures underwater and how to develop the pictures. That led to my need to take pictures above water and poof!—I was gone. I've been a diver all my life, but the reality is that photography really took my imagination and I just went on from there.

I had a neighbor, Harry Heinz, who gave me a little project to do for his church in the early sixties. And then he introduced me to a magical man, Merle Morris, who was not so much a people person, but a great mentor. And Merle and I had a four or five-year-long relationship, and he was great to me. He taught me how to have an eye, he taught me to look.

What defined you as a photographer when you were a young adult?

I think my enthusiasm defined who I was as a young photographer, because I don't think that I had the artistic ability. But I had the enthusiasm and I loved to take pictures. And there was something very special about taking pictures, about watching them develop in the first tray. The first tray is the developer, the second tray is stop bath, and the third tray is hypo. And then you rinse them and you have your prints. In a way, the first tray was always important to me. I kind of knew what I had in the camera, but then I got it into the enlarger and put it in the first tray. And then I really knew. And that's what captivated me, was seeing that image develop in that first tray, the developer tray.

What motivated your photography?

I think that my motivation as a photographer was a mix of desire and opportunity. Sometimes you can have the desire, and you simply don't have the opportunity. Sometimes you can have the opportunity, and you don't have the desire. But for me, I was lucky enough to have both in the sense that I had the desire, this burning desire to make images. And I also had a tremendous opportunity, in that I had a huge playground for me as a photographer. For example, I could use all of the equipment at Merle's and I could seek counsel from much wiser people. I went in there and dug out every ounce of opportunity I could to do what I wanted to do, which was make photos.

What inspires your photographer's eye today?

I think it's probably the discovery of my children. If I were to say one thing with my still camera, it would be to illustrate the encounters of my children with the world. Looking back over a small archive of these images, I think that I've done an adequate job of documenting their encounters with the world. But if there was one thing that I could call my passion, it would be to ask, "How do my children encounter the world?" I spent forty plus years as a child encountering the world, and recording it as a photographer. And now if I can record a little bit of how my children encounter the world, I think that's a pretty special recording session.

When your kids see this book, what do you want them to think or feel?

Very sensitive question. You know, the reality is, I hope that I've done much more in my life than this book. I'm really glad that people like this book, but the reality is I've got a lot more things in my life. And for my kids, I hope that the book just rests in the banker's box of stuff that they'll look through one day, and say, "Wow. Dad did a book," or "All of Dad's great associates came together and did this book." Because that's the way it's always been. It's not about Dad's film or Dad's book—it's about the great people who have come together and done something that means something to other people. I think that's the lesson I want to leave with my children, that no one person can do this. We do this as a team. We do this in love. We do this in passion for something—you can't do this alone.

When we delude ourselves into thinking that we can do something alone, we never really accomplish anything. And I think that's probably, maybe, the most important lesson I'd like to leave my kids with, is that you need to develop a team and develop a strategy. If you have a goal, work for it.

PRODUCER'S NOTE

As I was leafing through photographer Bill Carlson's high school yearbook recently, I was struck by the impressive volume of adoring female fans he had. The proof lies in the multiple entries that are peppered with the Hail Mary of flirtation—"I love your blue eyes." Notwithstanding my immature exercise of prying into the details of my husband's adolescence from 1966, I encountered an interesting revelation: each and every message written to Bill contained a expression of awe, admiration, respect, or gratitude—sometimes a combination of all four. Jeannie B. writes, "The photography is just marvelous. You've really done a great job on all you've set out to do this year. I am sure that you will continue to be a success in all you do, too." And then Mike T. asks, "How are you going to choose which talent to use, Bill?" Well, if I know Bill well (and I think I do), the answer is, he doesn't choose.

From cave diving, to racecar driving, to cinematography, Bill Carlson might be one of those ridiculously lucky people who are born with a passion, and ample talent to satisfy that passion. Beyond that, it seems that everything Bill touches in the course of exercising his passion leaves in its wake something magical and creative, an impression that leaves its object immeasurably better than before.

Bill was once a high school student who used his free time to flex his creative muscles with a camera. Couple that with the unusual reality that the 1965 Beatles concert was only an excuse and venue to do just that, and you see my point about how Bill's default is always to add, to gift, or to bring something special to someone else. That his book of photographs from just one day can touch so many people on so many levels is a testament to this involuntary characteristic of his, where his creative output becomes another's gift, as opposed to a mercenary addition to his own portfolio.

If you are holding this book, then you are likely a serious Beatles fan, just as dedicated today as those frenzied teens who once mobbed airports to catch a glimpse of the Fab Four as they touched ground. And I am just like them in my devotion, screaming with delight as John, Paul, Ringo, and George wave on. But my eye will be focused elsewhere. I will be gazing with unbridled love and admiration at the quiet one over there, the one behind the camera, the one in that racecar, and the one in that deep, dark cave with those amazing blue eyes.

DENISE GARDNER, BILL CARLSON'S #1 FAN

ABOUT THE AUTHOR

Bill Carlson was born in Minneapolis, Minnesota. From an early age, Bill was determined to follow in the footsteps of his hero, Jacques Cousteau. From the age of thirteen, Bill took the forty-five-minute bus ride across town to work in the St. Paul Dive shop, Midwest Skin Diving. It was there where his first mentor, diver Gene Betz, who also happened to be a commercial photographer, introduced Bill to what would become his twin passions, diving and photography. Several years later, Bill landed a job as a photographer for Merle Morris, an elite photographic studio in Minneapolis. After graduating from high school, Bill took his Nikons and portfolio and moved to Honolulu, Hawaii, where he worked in advertising photography and production. Assessing the arc of his career in photography, Bill is most proud of his still work from the refugee camps in Thailand and from the former Soviet Union, for which he was honored with a show at the Larson Gallery in Minneapolis.

Never one to follow conventions, Bill developed a taste for speed and pursued a career in car racing, while maintaining his ardor and livelihood as a photographer. Having raced all across North America, Bill's fifteen-year-long career in open-wheel formula cars, oval-track stock cars, and off-road competitions is a chapter he contemplates revisiting.

In the mid-80s, Bill made the transition from still photography to cinematography and has been the director of photography on numerous commercials, films, and documentaries. His clients include CNN, National Geographic, Canal Plus, France's TF1, Madrid's TVE, Japan's NHK, PBS, Coca Cola USA, Yamaha Motor Corporation, and American Express. His most recent project (2009) is the feature film *Pride of Lions*, a documentary about Sierra Leone and its 11-year-long civil war.

Active in scuba diving since 1958, Bill is also a PADI Dive master. Beyond his film work under the ice and in shipwrecks, he has been a trained cave diver since 1986, having extensive experience exploring and filming in the underwater cave systems of Mexico and northern Florida. He is a long-time member of the team credited with establishing the world record of explored underwater cave passage (43,800 feet), as recorded in the 1992 *Guinness Book of Records*. That record has been pushed to over 200,000 feet in recent explorations.

Bill currently resides with his family (Denise, Tomàs, and Elena) in Minnesota, where he navigates the bays of Lake Minnetonka in his 1957 Cadillac runabout. His most recent project (2009) is the feature film Pride of Lions, a documentary about Sierra Leone and its 11-year-long civil war.